"We have used Dr. Keim's *'Keys To Success In College and Life'* for four years at Iowa State University with all our incoming new students. It is an outstanding orientation and retention resource written by a person who knows students as well as anyone in our nation! It has made a significant contribution to helping students make the transition to college. I recommend it to every student, their parents, and their university's first year program."

—*Dr. Tom Hill*
Vice President of Student Life
Iowa State University
Olympic Medalist, Track & Field

Keys to
Success

Books by Will Keim, Ph.D.:

Fan Etiquette: How Did the Burning Desire
  to Win Become the Desire to Burn?
The Education of Character
Spirit Journey
The Tao of Christ
The Truth About College
Life After College
Wit & Wisdom
Demythologizing the Animal House
Welcome To The Time of Your Life
La Verdad Sobre Colegio (The Truth About College)
authors Jesus JamieDiaz, Henry Villegas, Norma Valenzuela, Ph:D.
& Will Keim, Ph.D

Co-Authored by Dr. Will Keim

Let Your Leadership Speak:
  How to Lead and Be Heard
Chicken Soup for the College Soul
Leadership's Greatest Hits
Pillars of Success; by Keim, Haig, Summit, et.al.
Speaking of Success; by Keim, Covey, Tracy, et. al.
Roadmap to Success; by Keim, Chopra, Blanchard, et. al.

Books by Curtis Zimmerman:
I Believe … What Do You Believe?
Living Life at Performance Level
Co-Authored to:
Leadership's Greatest Hits

Coming in 2013 from Viaticum Press:
The Playbook for Life: The Real
  Meaning of Success for Student
  Athletes, Athletic Administrators,
  and Coach Educators

Keys to Success In High School & Life,
by Askew, Harlan, Hartley, Laippley,
Diaz, Villegas, Zimmerman, Schmeder,
& Keim

For information about booking Will Keim or Curtis Zimmerman to visit your campus, contact one of the following:

Will Keim Speaks!, Inc.
3850 NW Jackson
Corvallis, OR 97330
(541) 740-1318
www.willkeim.com

Curtis Zimmerman Group
7577 Central Parke Blvd., Suite 217
Mason, OH 45040
(513) 229-3626
www.curtiszimmerman.com

E-mail IDs:
willkeim@willkeim.com, curtis@curtiszimmerman.com

This book and other Viaticum Press CDs, DVDs, and VHS resources may be purchased at special group pricing for educational uses. Contact Viaticum Press. The first edition of *Keys to Success* was published in August 2003 by The Character Institute and authored by Will Keim, Ph.D., and Curtis Zimmerman. "Ten Strategic Study Success Steps," "Ten Characteristics of Effective Leadership," and "Fifty Stress Busters For Students" were previously published by Viaticum Press. Copyright © 2004 by Will Keim, Ph.D. Reprinted with permission.

ISBN 0-9631834-8-6

Second Edition

Keys to
Success

in College and Life

Will Keim, Ph.D.
Curtis Zimmerman

VIATICUM PRESS
CORVALLIS, OREGON
MASON, OHIO

"To laugh often and much;
to win the respect of intelligent
people and the affection
of children; to earn the
appreciation of honest critics
and endure the betrayal of false
friends; to appreciate beauty,
to find the best in others;
to leave the world a little better;
whether by a healthy child,
a garden patch or a redeemed
social condition; to know even
one life has breathed easier
because you have lived. This is
the meaning of success. "

—*Ralph Waldo Emerson*
1803 – 1882
Poet and philosopher

Introduction

> ❝ **Never give up.**
> **Never ever give up.** ❞
>
> *—Jim Valvano*
> *1946 – 1993*
> *Basketball coach*

Curtis Zimmerman has a "Masters in Life" degree from the School of Hard Knocks. Will Keim earned his first college degree because he knew how to throw a curve ball. The two of us are as different as can be; however, we're all tenacious. We wouldn't quit, and we were like junk-yard dogs in pursuit of success. Curtis became one of America's most respected mimes, entertaining millions on television, at Universal Studios, and on Carnival Cruise Lines. Will finished his Ph.D. at Oregon State University while teaching three speech classes, being a residence hall director, and starting a family with his wife, Donna. He has lectured to more than two million students from 2,000 universities. Yes, our collective resume highlights are reasonably spectacular:

Authors of eleven books
Juggler
Jack Anson Award, Association for Fraternity Advisors
Carnival Cruise Lines headliner
NCAA Recognized Speakers
Rotary Foundation Fellow
Universal Studios Entertainer of the Year
Durwood Owen Award Recipient
Delta Upsilon Outstanding Alumni Award
Fire Eater
Paul Harris Fellow
Seven children among us
Keynote Speaker United States Air Force Character &
     Leadership Symposium
Keynote Speaker National Forum on Character
Four-year Division I Varsity Letterman
Ph.D., M.A., B.A. with Honors
Consultant to Fortune 500 companies

But before we go on together toward success, you should know our "real-sumes" as well. "Real-sumes" is our own, made-up word for a hard look at our real lives. Here are just some of the things that happened to at least one of us:

Mom married six times
Stepdad was an alcoholic
Sexually abused as a child
37 trips to hospital before age 9
Welfare and food stamps growing up
Problem drinking
Nearly died of asthma attack
Parents and stepparents married 14 times
Disease-causing seizures
Dyslexia
Had four children in intense care neo-natal ward

Okay, we know what *we've* done. We are more concerned with what *you* will do with your life. We do not want you to feel sorry for us, and we do not want to feel sorry for you. Rather, we want us and you to become better people every day. So, this is a book about hope and possibilities. It is about becoming a better student, a more considerate friend, an effective leader and a healthy person — physically and mentally. We want you to know that it is also tempered with realism.

Some of you may breeze through some chapters because you already have the subject wired. If you have great parents, Character Lesson 8, about letting go of your anger towards your parents, won't take much time. If you are a brainiac, then our advice on scholarship in Character Lesson 1 may be something you already know. There is, however, a gem, a tidbit, and an insight in each chapter. It is very important that you complete the exercises in each lesson. Do not skip or "blow off" the material. If it is in this book, then we believe it's important.

We welcome you to *Keys to Success* and hope passionately that "The 12 Character Lessons" will help you move in a positive direction as you begin your collegiate journey.

Blessings,
Dr. Will Keim and Curtis Zimmerman

Contents

Foreword by Susan Scott. 7

Lesson 1: Scholarship. 9

Lesson 2: Service 17

Lesson 3: Peacemaking. .23

Lesson 4: Character 29

Lesson 5: Health 33

Lesson 6: Spirit 39

Lesson 7: Freedom 45

Lesson 8: Letting Go. 53

Lesson 9: The Secret. 59

Lesson 10: 25,000 Days .65

Lesson 11: Living Life at Performance Level. 73

Lesson 12: Learning to Fail Successfully 79

Put it all together: Review/Resources 85

Foreword

Wow! If I had read this book when I started college:

I might not have had a rough time in the campus clinic my freshman year discovering that you can become seriously dehydrated from drinking too much alcohol.

I would have changed roommates quicker and been lots happier.

I would have been comforted to know others had the same questions and concerns I had.

Will Keim and Curtis Zimmerman have addressed students' most pressing questions and concerns in this terrific book. Their experience with millions of students on college campuses across the nation has enabled them to nail the issues in language any college student can understand.

If you are headed to college, read this book.

—Susan Scott
Author, *Fierce Conversations: Achieving Success at Work and In Life—One Conversation at a Time*

> "Learn all you can from the mistakes of others. You won't have time to make them all yourself."
>
> —*Alfred Sheinwold*
> *1912 – 1997*
> *Playwright*

Scholarship

> **The world cares very little about what a man or woman knows; it is what the man or woman is able to do that counts.**
>
> *—Booker T. Washington*
> *1856 – 1915*
> *Author and activist*

Traveling Man

Because of his struggles with dyslexia, Curtis spent most of his formal education in special education classes. In junior high, he met Norma Natale, a caring teacher, mentor, and world traveler. With her love and teaching abilities, she brought Curtis up nearly three grade levels in one year. After his high school graduation ceremony, Curtis came home to find four pieces of Polo luggage with a note that simply read: "Curtis, thank you for being one of the few students to ever graduate from my classes. I know you will travel the world as an amazing entertainer, and I thought you should go in style. Your friend and teacher, Norma."

Norma was right. Curtis traveled the world, including the Caribbean, Alaska, and the Mexican Riviera, on Carnival and Regency cruise lines as a professional entertainer. He wore out that luggage, but he never forgot the impact that one caring teacher had on one student, named "Curtis."

Who is the "Norma Natale" in your life?

Will speaks:

"A few years ago, I visited the University of Tennessee to speak to the student athletes. The women's basketball team was seated in the front row. I asked them, "How come y'all sit right up front?" One of the players, Semeka Randall, smiled and said, "Because Coach Pat Summitt tells us to sit in the front of the classroom, in the front of the lecture, in the front of the movies, so we get used to being in front of things like the NCAA.'

"That basketball team *did* win the NCAA national championship. Semeka Randall now plays professional basketball in the WNBA and is an assistant coach at Michigan State University."
Sit in the front of the class.

—*Will Keim*

The basic assumption of this character lesson is simple yet profound: You are setting the banquet table now for the feast you will eat the rest of your life. Scholarship is the primary key that starts the vehicle in which you will negotiate your post-college plans: graduate school, salary, and career. Or NOT.

You must envision yourself graduating with your diploma in one hand and your self-esteem in the other hand. Students do not plan to fail. Rather, they fail to plan.

Being a good student is the basis on which success must be built. All of us will earn our living with what we learn in the classroom and in co-curricular activities.

Visualization Exercise

Imagine your college graduation day. Is it sunny? What time of day is the ceremony? Where is it? Where would you like to go afterward to celebrate? List the people you want to be there:

66 **The journey of a thousand miles begins beneath your feet.** 99

—*Lao Tzu*
Sixth century, B.C.
Father of Taoism

_____

_____

_____

_____

_____

Ten Strategic Study Success Steps

1. Sit in the front row or up close.
2. Take notes in every class.
3. After class, recopy your notes in outline form.
4. Get a syllabus from every instructor.
5. Make a master syllabus of all assignments (see examples on the next two pages).
6. Read all assignments.
7. Study on road trips.
8. Pick a study partner.
9. Study between classes.
10. Meet the professor, ask questions, and go to the professor's office hours if you need help.

Keep track

We believe that if you have one place to check on assignments, then there is a much greater chance you can stay on top of what you need to do. On the following two pages, we've provided charts to help you organize your academic workload. Keep track by topic or by assignment — your choice.

> " Education worthy of the name is essentially the education of character. "
>
> —*Martin Buber*
> *1875-1965*
> *Philosopher*

Meagan Denney speaks:

"I had big shoulders and I didn't fee good about myself. In addition, I had a learning disability. I could not get the work done as fast as the other children in the class. 'She's in the special class' they would say when I walked by. Then I found a teacher who would design tests to help me show my knowledge of the subject matter. My parents never gave up on me. At that time I discovered I could throw a softball and throw it fast. Suddenly, I was popular and began to feel better about myself. My grades improved too. I went to the University of Texas on an athletic scholarship. Now I play professional softball and speak for Dr. Will Keim's Higher Aspirations. Find a mentor. Believe in yourself."

Ask questions. You can do it.

—*Meagan Denney*

Master Syllabus Option #1: By Topic

Write in your assignments for every class.

Day/Week/Month	Reading Assignments	Papers	Presentations & Speeches	Labs	Mid Term	Final

Master Syllabus Option #2: By Class

Write in your assignments for every class.

Class 1		Class 2		Class 3		Class 4		Class 5	
Due		Due		Due		Due		Due	

Assignment: Set your academic goals

At the beginning of the term, write down a realistic goal for each class and an action plan to achieve that goal. At the end of the term, revisit the goals you set. Were you successful? Why? Why not? Be honest with yourself. You are on your way with a plan for academic success.

Class	Desired Grade and Action Plan	Actual Grade	Most Valuable Lesson Learned
Example: Speech 101	*Grade: A. Attend every class. Read all assignments. Practice speeches.*	*A. Accomplished goal!*	*Practice was key to good public speaking.*

**If you are having academic difficulty,
talk to your:**

- ❏ **Faculty Advisor**
- ❏ **Resident Assistant**
- ❏ **Professor**
- ❏ **Dean of Students**
- ❏ **Parent**
- ❏ **Coach**
- ❏ **Teammate**
- ❏ **Academic Success Counselor**

> It is wise to keep in mind that no success or failure is necessarily final.
>
> —*Anonymous*

Tip: Pick more than one. You don't have to do it alone.

M&Ms

"Maximize the Missing Minutes" (M&Ms) is our way to help you use your time wisely. Study during the day between classes. You will pick up an additional 2–4 hours of high-quality study time per day. Go to the library, a coffee shop, or wherever you prefer to study.

Combine M&Ms with "Ten Strategic Study Success Tips" (earlier in this chapter), and you will be well on your way to achieving academic success.

Your Passion

We believe that you should choose a major that truly reflects something that you are deeply passionate about. It should lead to a profession that you can willingly and with joy spend one half of your waking hours pursuing. Character Lesson 9 offers you an opportunity to discover your passion and begin the process of selecting a major that becomes your life's work.

Will you choose:

a Diploma	or	an Education?
a Workout	or	a Healthy Lifestyle?
a Date	or	a Relationship?
an Idea	or	a Dream?
a Job	or	a Vocation?

The first options are good, but the second options are better!

Character Lesson 2

Service

> **You can't live a perfect day without doing something for someone who will never be able to repay you.**
>
> —*John Wooden*
> *1910 –*
> *College basketball coach*

Mentoring others

A bus pulled up in front of the Boys and Girls Club in Camas, Washington. As the children happily lined up to board the bus, an interested passerby asked, "Where are you going?" One little girl giggled excitedly and said, "We're going with the DU guys. They're fun." The Boys and Girls Club director, seeing the quizzical look on the man's face, explained: "We're headed to the Delta Upsilon fraternity leadership center in Portland. Everyone had so much fun last week, we're doing it again!" They played ball and tag, juggled, threw footballs, and played pool. A three-hour community-service project had resulted in new friendships. Three hours and everyone wanted to do it again. Three hours and a group of children now had a group of young men to look up to—mentors. Every time you serve someone else, somehow your own problems are put in perspective. The small bathroom shared with two roommates is no big deal compared to the beat-up station wagon the kid at the club calls home. The cafeteria chicken is delicious when compared to the peanut-butter sandwich the child will eat today at the club—his only meal of the day. We should all count our blessings, and share them with others.

Service

Scholarship

Meagan Denney speaks:

"Whenever we play a professional softball tournament, we do a clinic for little girls who want to be softball players. I love to go to their games on Sundays after we play Friday and Saturday nights and watch them play and support them. Everything we give to the girls comes back to us tenfold in a smile, a laugh, or a look of self-confidence from their beautiful faces. In serving others you yourself are served with a greater gift. In giving, we receive."

Living is giving.

—*Meagan Denney*
PFX Professional Softball Team
Inspirational Speaker

Time Out.

Before you decide to volunteer, join a club, become a reporter, go Greek, try out for a team, become a resident assistant, take 19 credit hours, or work 30 hours while you take a full course load, let's call "TIME OUT" and assess your strengths and weaknesses.

On your mark.
Choose a good attitude.
Show up.
Be on time.
Be prepared.
Work hard

Get set.
Analyze your strengths.
Identify your weaknesses.
Be honest and kind with
yourself.

Go.
To breakfast.
To class.
To practice.
To the library.
To the career center.
To a spiritual place.
To campus programs.
TO BED
(6-8 hours of sleep
per night).

Your schedule makes us tired!
Get some rest.

> **Seventy percent of success in life is showing up.**
>
> —*Woody Allen*
> *1935 –*
> *Film director and actor*

Who are you?

How well do you know yourself?
Do your friends know you?
Let's take an inventory.

Four words I use to describe me:

_____   _____

_____   _____

Four words my friends use to describe me:

_____   _____

_____   _____

Do the lists match? If not, why?

My top three strengths:

_____

_____

_____

Three weaknesses I have:

_____

_____

_____

If I could change one thing about myself, it would be:

_____

_____

_____

Three of my talents or skills that could be useful to others:

_____

_____

_____

Time In.

❝Will Keim is committed to excellence and someone you can trust, who really cares about you. When he speaks, we all should listen.❞

—*Lou Holtz*
1937 –
College football coach

Will speaks:

"I was thrilled to see Lou Holtz, one of the winningest coaches in college football, in the Crown Room at Delta Air Lines in Atlanta. I said, 'Hello coach, I don't want to bother you, but we are both in the same fraternity.' He said hello and shook my hand. I continued, 'I'm at a point in my career where I need someone famous to say something nice about me.' He said, 'Mail me a tape. I'd love to help you.' A week later he sent a wonderful quote that opened many doors for me (and we used it on this page). He mentored me. He didn't have to. He's just that kind of man…a mentor and a friend. I am honored to call him my brother. I hope you have a mentor."

Find a mentor.

—*Will Keim*

Wisdom on finding a mentor

Warren G. Bennis is a Distinguished Professor of Business Administration at the University of Southern California. He also serves as the Thomas S. Murphy Distinguished Research Scholar at Harvard Business School. He has written twenty-five books on leadership and change. Here is some of his advice:

> **"While the popular view of mentors is that they seek out younger people to encourage and champion, in fact the reverse is true. The best mentors are usually recruited, and one mark of a future leader is the ability to identify, woo, and win the mentors who will change his or her life."**

You would be wise to heed his wisdom and recruit a mentor. No one is an island and the "self-made man or woman" is a myth. Seek a mentor to guide and encourage your journey.

New Students and Sophomores

Identify someone who is older, or perhaps wiser, who might serve as a mentor to you. Don't be afraid to ask—be assertive, direct and honest.

Juniors and Seniors

Choose an underclass student whom you will make an effort to mentor as a protege. Be honored if someone asks you to be a mentor.

Commit yourself to one hour a week to talk, e-mail, visit, or hang out with each other.

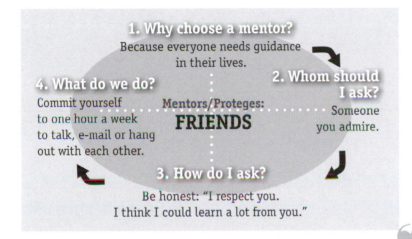

1. Why choose a mentor?
Because everyone needs guidance in their lives.

2. Whom should I ask?
Someone you admire.

3. How do I ask?
Be honest: "I respect you. I think I could learn a lot from you."

4. What do we do?
Commit yourself to one hour a week to talk, e-mail or hang out with each other.

Mentors/Proteges:
FRIENDS

> We can do no great things. Only small things with great love.
>
> —*Mother Teresa*
> *1910 – 1997*
> *Catholic nun and social activist*

The act of giving

By now it should be obvious to you that we believe good character includes service, and that great learning takes place in the act of giving assistance to others. Mentoring is just one way to be of service.

As Mother Teresa said, we can do "small things with great love" and inspire others to join us in the effort. Nothing puts your problems in perspective better than helping others in their time of need. It is always wise to follow the Golden Rule, because what you "do unto others" may eventually "be done unto you."

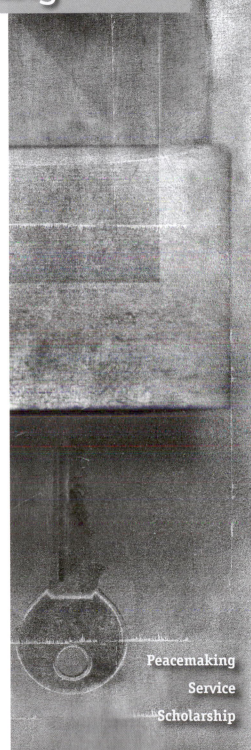

Character Lesson 3 — Peacemaking

> **An eye for an eye and a tooth for a tooth results in a blind, toothless world.**
>
> —*Golda Meier*
> *1898 – 1978*
> *Israeli political leader*

Putting the 'Civil' back in Civil War

The annual in-state rivalry football game between the University of Oregon and Oregon State University is called the Civil War. The crowd behavior, however, had a history of being anything but civil. After two years of extraordinarily rude and obnoxious home crowds at the popular event, the fraternities and sororities at both schools founded "Put the Civil Back in Civil War." Students, athletes, cheerleaders, and student leaders from both schools began to visit elementary schools together in each town. Side by side, they talk about resolving conflict without violence. Each elementary school receives a $500 check for school supplies from the rival university. The mascots shake hands, and the children see cooperation and friendship. Since the inception of the program, civility has increased and the crowds have respected each other with little or no problems. Peacemaking can be taught and can be learned. Would a program like this work at your school and its rival?

Peacemaking

Service

Scholarship

> **Will speaks:**
>
> "From reading the title of this chapter, you may have thought that this lesson was about making peace in the world. That is certainly a good idea, and it is much needed today. We, however, are talking about making peace with yourself.
>
> "In 1998 I heard Dr. Parker Palmer, a well-known writer, teacher, and activist, speak in St. Louis. He said something so profound that I carry it with me to this day. What he said was this: 'People will live divided no more when they realize that no punishment anyone could lay on them is worse than what they are laying on themselves by conspiring in their own diminishment.'"
> **Make peace with yourself.**
>
> —*Will Keim*

> If there is to be peace
> in the world,
> There must be peace
> in the nations.
> If there is to be peace
> in the nations,
> There must be peace
> in the cities.
> If there is to be peace
> in the cities,
> There must be peace
> between neighbors.
> If there is to be peace
> between neighbors,
> There must be peace
> in the home.
> If there is to be peace
> in the home,
> There must be peace
> in the heart.
>
> —*Lao Tzu*
> *Sixth century, B.C.*
> *Father of Taoism*

Are you a conspirator in your own diminishment? Do your actions bring people closer to you, or push them away? Do you live divided between the person you wish you were or want to be and the person you really are?

We believe it is completely possible to "live divided no more." You can change, become integrated, and be at peace with yourself.

Albert Einstein observed, "One definition of insanity is doing the same thing over and over again and expecting a different result."

Change is not the enemy. You are not the enemy. In order to make peace with yourself, you must ask yourself some serious questions in moments of quiet reflection.

Good starter questions:

- Who am I?
- Why am I here?
- What is my purpose?
- What are my greatest gifts?
- What do I have to offer?
- What gives my life meaning?
- What do I believe in?

These questions rest in every soul, and sadly, some people never ask them nor search for the answers.

Once you begin on the path of making peace with yourself, then you may desire to make peace and resolve conflict with others.

Our goal is simple: civility between people, groups, religions, nations—civility on earth—doing what's right. Civility is treating others as you would like to be treated. Let's look at ways to reach ethical decisions and a methodology to handle conflict interpersonally, rather than angrily or violently.

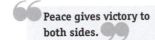

> **Peace gives victory to both sides.**
>
> —*Ralph Waldo Emerson*
> *1803 – 1882*
> *Poet and philosopher*

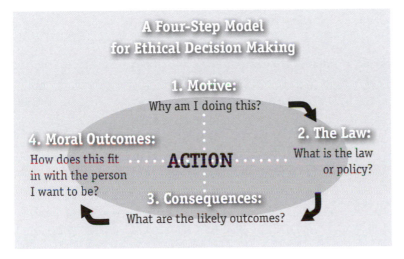

A Four-Step Model for Ethical Decision Making

1. Motive: Why am I doing this?

2. The Law: What is the law or policy?

3. Consequences: What are the likely outcomes?

4. Moral Outcomes: How does this fit in with the person I want to be?

ACTION

Ask:

1. Why?
2. Is it legal?
3. What could happen?
4. Is it moral?

Think before you act.

Bottom line: Is it right? Is this action consistent with my values and beliefs? Then, and only then, do the deed.

Conflicts are a normal part of life. Sporting events are organized conflict within a set of established rules and plays. It is *how* we handle conflict that matters most.

If you have a disagreement with a parent, professor, boyfriend, or girlfriend, then follow this five-step model to resolve conflict interpersonally:

A Five-Step Model
for Handling Conflict Interpersonally

Step 1: Be specific.
Step 2: Avoid blaming and moralizing.
Step 3: Talk one to one.
Step 4: Talk in a nonstressful place and time.
Step 5: Leave an open door.

1 **When you have a conflict, be specific.** "You were a flaming idiot" is interesting but not helpful. "When we stopped them on fourth down and one, and you got a taunting penalty, it really hurt the team" is very direct and specific.

2 **Avoid blaming and moralizing.** "We lost because of you," "It's your fault," and "If you continue to drink you will burn in hell" are not bridge-builders. "I have a problem." "What's your problem?" "I have a problem with your drinking" works much better.

3 **Talk one to one.** Public arguments turn into theater, and we often say things we don't mean just to "win" the argument in front of others. It's quite possible to "win" an argument and lose a friend.

4 **Talk in a nonstressful place and time.** Calm down before you heat up. Call a personal "time out," walk away, agree to disagree. Rarely has stress, alcohol, or anger helped resolve anything. Stress, alcohol, and anger can dissolve, not resolve, relationships.

5 **Leave an open door.** That means never bringing the disagreement to an end with statements like: "That's it. We're done. It's over." "Get out of here. I never want to see you again." Or "I'll never change my mind, so we should just go our separate ways." Instead, tell your friend you will talk about it later.

> **All humanity is one undivided and indivisible family, and each one of us is responsible for the misdeeds of all the others.**
>
> *— Mahatma Gandhi*
> *1869 – 1948*
> *Idealist*

Think about a conflict in your life. It could be with a roommate, a parent, a professor, or a friend. Using the list below, describe how you might handle the situation. Refer to the list at left for examples.

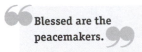

Blessed are the peacemakers.

—Jesus of Nazareth
First century, A.D.

1   Describe the conflict in specific terms:

_____

_____

_____

2   Write a statement about the conflict
that does not blame or moralize:

_____

_____

_____

3   Specify a setting where you could
discuss the conflict privately:

_____

_____

_____

4   Describe how this setting and time will
not contribute to the stress of the discussion:

_____

_____

5   Write an example of a statement that
will leave an open door between the two of you:

_____

_____

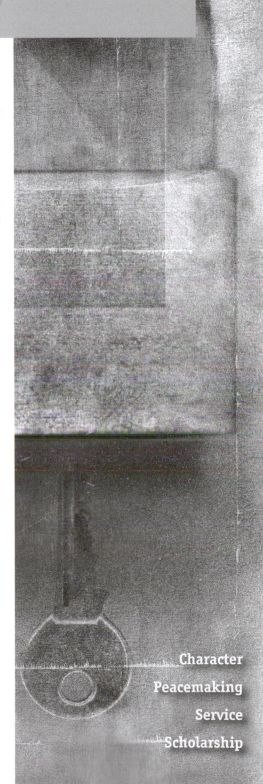

Character Lesson 4

Character

> ❝I hope I shall always possess firmness and virtue enough to maintain what I consider the most enviable of all titles: the character of an honest man.❞
>
> *—George Washington*
> *1732 – 1799*
> *First President of the United States*

When no one is looking

"Our character is what we do when we think no one is looking," said the author and philosopher H. Jackson Browne. While lecturing at the University of Kentucky, Will mentioned that Megan Jones, one of the gymnasts at Oregon State University, had been hit and seriously injured by a drunk driver. Will asked the Kentucky gymnasts if they would have the time to send her a get-well card. One of them said, "We already did, Dr. Keim. Gymnastics is like a family, and we prayed for Megan and sent her a card." This didn't make the Lexington newspapers but it did make an impression on Will.

Character

Peacemaking

Service

Scholarship

Tondaleya Jackson speaks:

"Three men were chasing me in their car as I drove to my work when I was younger. The two passengers were filled with hate and their words were intensely derogatory and dissed my color and my gender. I was afraid. The driver looked different and in his eyes I could see someone who knew this wasn't right. I thank God that he drove off and took the frightening passengers with him. I saw compassion, character, and regret in the driver's eyes and face. What do you do when no one is looking? You may never know how important your individual actions may be. The driver pulled away and saved me hurt, and perhaps even violence. We're not talking about the '60s here. It was the early '90s."

We have work to do.

—*Tondaleya Jackson*
Total Learning Concepts
South Carolina

Character is who you are when no one is watching. A world of integrity and character begins with one person at a time knowing and acting on this adage:

Say what you mean. Do what you say.
If you don't, admit it. Make amends, and move on.

Your own model

Let's build your own model for character: Fill in each line with a word that begins with the letters of "character." Take your pick from the list below or come up with your own words. Your list will represent what character means to you.

> **All of your scholarship, all your study of Shakespeare and Wordsworth would be in vain if at the same time you did not build your character and attain mastery over your thoughts and your actions.**
>
> — *Mahatma Gandhi*
> *1869 – 1948*
> *Idealist*

C _____

H _____

A _____

R _____

A _____

C _____

T _____

E _____

R _____

Some suggestions:

Caring. Coaching. Cooperative.
Courageous. Charismatic.
Compassionate. Committed. Candid.
Humorous. Humble. Hearing.
Helpful. Happy. Action-oriented.
Accommodating. Appreciative.
Respectful. Responsible. Renowned.
Responsive. Relatable. Teaching.
Trusting. Tutor. Team-focused.
Empathic. Empowering. Energetic.
Exciting.
Be creative!

Character in person

Name someone you know who has a good character and
list his or her characteristics:

I admire _____because

_____

_____

_____

Character in the workplace

List your desired professions or jobs in Column 1. Write down three
to five. In Column 2, write down the characteristics needed to do
those jobs well. In Column 3, list the characteristics of successful
organizations that would offer these jobs. What are the connections?

Profession or Job	Characteristics Needed to Do this Profession or Job	Characteristics of a Successful Organization
Example: Newspaper foreign correspondent	*Courageous. Curious. Honest. Good listener. Observant. Open minded.*	*Honest. Cooperative. Committed. Responsible. Team focused. Appreciative.*

Health

> **If you want to solve the world's problems, you have to put your own household, your own individual life in order first.**
>
> —*Chögyam Trungpa*
> *1939 – 1987*
> *Teacher and meditation master*

Gold medals for sex?

Dr. Robin Sawyer is a wonderful teacher and researcher at the University of Maryland. His expertise is public health with a focus on human sexuality. Dr. Sawyer is English, witty, and the husband and father that wives and children dream of having. He says, "If sex were an Olympic sport, the United States would have all the gold medals." Before Americans gloat about medals, Dr. Sawyer goes on to clarify. Of the 13 industrialized nations, the United States is ranked:

- #1 in unwanted pregnancies
- #1 in sexually transmitted diseases (STDs)
- #1 in acquisition of HIV
- #1 in genital herpes

Guess we really don't want those gold medals after all.

Health
Character
Peacemaking
Service
Scholarship

Curtis speaks:

"Real words don't always capture what I mean or would like to say, so sometimes I make up words. 'Response-Able' is one of my favorite sayings. 'Being Response-Able' means being able to stop, consider your options, and then make the right choice. When it comes to alcohol, drugs and sex, saying 'no' is often the most Response-Able thing to do, and clearly the safest, most ethical and legal thing to do as well."

Be Response-Able.

—*Curtis Zimmerman*

> **Never continue in a job you don't enjoy. If you're happy in what you're doing, you'll like yourself, you'll have inner peace. And if you have that, along with physical health, you will have had more success than you could possibly have imagined.**

—*Johnny Carson*
1925 – 2005
Entertainer

Prescription for Healthy Living

Take seven goals:

1. Drink alcohol Response-Ably*
2. Live drug free*
3. Practice Response-Able sexuality*
4. Perform at your academic best
5. Promote personal wellness
6. Exhibit community-minded behavior
7. Be tolerant and respectful.

* *Understand that saying "no" is often the most Response-Able thing to do.*

Mix with seven success tips:

1. Respect yourself and others.
2. Set your academic and personal agenda early.
3. Don't be afraid to fail or succeed.
4. Take care of yourself and others.
5. Accept the challenge college offers.
6. Listen to the "Voice" within.
7. Find something you love to do and learn to do it well enough that someone will pay you to do it.

Refine • Personalize • Take daily

Making the case for abstention

We've known a lot of great relationships ruined by sex and some bad relationships prolonged by it. Be honest with yourself. Virginity and self-control are not a curse. If you choose to be sexually active, consult a campus health educator and practice safer sex. Sex is never safe. Call us old-fashioned, but we would like to make the case for abstention. Not having sex is a great way *not* to get pregnant. You have little chance of acquiring HIV, and it limits the acquisition of herpes and other sexually transmitted diseases.

Men should treat women the way they would like their little sisters treated. And women should treat men the way they would like their little brothers treated.

Respect yourself. Respect others.

- Women and men should know that they will get the respect they command.
- Men and women who sleep around generally don't go home with anyone for Thanksgiving.
- Sex doesn't always include love and intimacy.
- Practice respect and you'll get it right back atcha!

> " True friendship is like sound health. The value of it is seldom known until it be lost. "
>
> —Rev. Charles Caleb Colton
> 1780 – 1832
> Author

Kaylee speaks:

"I was out dancing and my date handed me a drink. Shortly thereafter I began to feel woozy and light headed. I was short of breath and felt faint. I soon realized that I had been drugged. Three men began to take me out of the club when a police car happened by. I yelled, 'I need help', and the police stopped and took me to a hospital. I had been club drugged and was lucky to have escaped serious harm. I did suffer partial memory loss for several months but am thankful I was not assaulted. Be careful. Don't let someone take advantage of you. Go out with friends and at your first awareness of a problem, get help."

—Kaylee E.
Friend of Dr. Will Keim

Making healthy choices
is a matter of life and death

Based on several studies, the National Institute on Alcohol Abuse and Alcoholism estimates the following consequences of excessive and underage drinking for college students ages 18-24:

- 1,400 deaths per year
- 70,000 victims of sexual assault or rape
- 110,000 arrests related to alcohol
- 150,000 people with alcohol-related health problems
- 500,000 injuries
- 600,000 assaults
- 400,000 students had unprotected sex
- 100,000 students were too drunk to know if they consented to sex
- 2.1 million students drove while drunk
- 1.2% of students attempted suicide while drunk
- 11% committed acts of vandalism while drunk

Don't be a statistic. Be a graduate.

Practicing wellness is a smart lifestyle choice, perhaps your most important short- and long-term decision.

Club and designer drugs

Club and designer drugs sound quite benign, when in reality students are dropping dead and dropping their standards because of them. Medical doctor Michael Finley advises, "Even one use of club or designer drugs, especially Ecstasy, severely limits the brain's ability to produce serotonin, which is essential to the brain's ability to remember things. These drugs are not benign, they are neurotoxins."

- If you don't know what these drugs are: Great!
- If you don't know what they can do: Great Danger!
- It is time for you to educate yourself about Rohypnol, GHB, DXM, Ecstasy, and Ketamine.

Do not leave a drink unattended
at a social gathering at college.

Because some club drugs are colorless, tasteless, and odorless, individuals who want to intoxicate or sedate others can add them unobtrusively to beverages or food. In recent years, there has been an

increase in reports of club drugs used to commit sexual assaults, and for that reason they are referred to as "date rape drugs."
Source: National Institute on Drug Abuse

The subject of alcohol and other drugs is so important that we'll talk more about it in Character Lesson 7.

> *The healthy, the strong individual, is the one who asks for help when he needs it —whether he has an abscess on his knee or in his soul.*
>
> —Rona Barrett
> 1936 –
> Gossip columnist

Will speaks:

"I am an intercollegiate chaplain. Most students I've had the misfortune to bury were victims of alcohol- and drug-related incidents. Until you've seen the pain you cannot imagine the suffering."

Think. Abstain. Remember.

—*Will Keim*

Name four people to whom you could bring a problem (Sister? Brother? Best friend? Teammate? Mom? Dad? Grandma? Counselor? Resident assistant? Coach? Professor?)

_____   _____

_____   _____

List a few healthy choices you'd like to make this year:

_____

_____

_____

_____

_____

Healthy mind + Healthy body = Healthy spirit
Let your spirit soar.

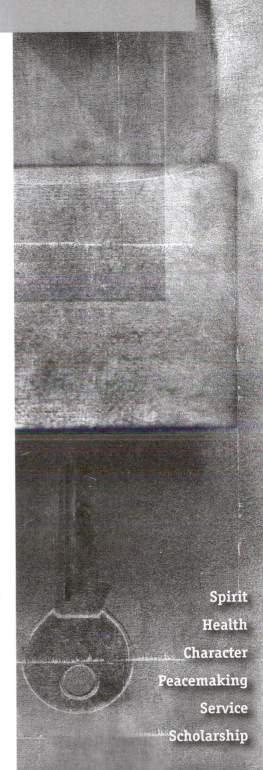

Character Lesson 6

Spirit

> **One truth stands firm. All that happens in world history rests on something spiritual. If the spirit is strong, it creates world history. If it is weak, it suffers world history.**
>
> —*Albert Schweitzer*
> *1875 – 1965*
> *Doctor and humanitarian*

My Mother, My Friend

"I saw my Mother the last time on a rainy morning in Oregon. She had been ill and suffering from dementia. We had kept her at home until the very end when her need for care exceeded our ability to provide it. My wife Donna had been a saint with her; bathing her, brushing her hair, making sure she ate and stayed home…even cutting her finger and toe nails. It was sad to see my Mother like that and equally inspiring to see Donna care for her as if she were her own Mom.

Bettye, my Mother, was irritated that morning and not resting well. She was not awake but struggled as if she knew the end was near. I held her hand and said, 'Mama, you can relax. We love you. God loves you. You don't have to be afraid. Let go and let God." I kissed her and told the nurse I would return after the morning's errands. I kissed her cheek and she calmed down immediately.

She died a short while later. She went peacefully and I miss her every day. I believe I will see her again. What do you believe? My friend Geoffrey Canada of the Harlem Children's Zone says, "The thing about faith is that you have to have it before you need it." It was comforting to have a spiritual place to go in my life that morning. And I think Mr. Canada is right."

Will Keim

Spirit

Health

Character

Peacemaking

Service

Scholarship

> **Curtis speaks:**
> "If you ever want to be a leader, you must know what you believe. All the great leaders in history had very strong belief systems and were willing to share their beliefs and dreams with others."
> **What do you believe?**
>
> —*Curtis Zimmerman*

Discovering your spirituality

Spirituality is about things unseen, but felt most profoundly. It is called by many names, but it all has to do with our search for meaning, the Higher Self, the Creator, the Source of All That Is.

We are not preaching religion. We are talking about spirituality, about knowing a presence in life that transcends what we can feel, touch, smell, taste, or eat. Collegiate life is a wonderful time to discover or rediscover your own personal spirituality. Especially around midterms —there are a lot of people praying about those.

Billy Mills, the Native American Olympic gold medallist, tells about a Lakota tradition of holding a child up facing the heavens and saying to the little one, "Behold the only thing greater than yourself."

Professor Diana Eck of Harvard University defines "spirituality" as "real religion that touches the heart." The religious writer Rabbi Kushner adds, "Our tolerance of others' spirituality is a direct barometer of our own spiritual security."

Some define their spirituality as a belief in God. Some use different words. Twelve Step programs say "Higher Power." Lakotas say "Wakantanka." Others say "Allah," "Ishvara," "Tao," or "Jehovah." The choice is yours.

When we talk of spirituality, we are talking about solid values and beliefs that will help every student grow and achieve his or her own peace. We are talking about:

- Compassion
- Love
- Tolerance
- Patience
- Kindness

> **Always do right. This will gratify some people and astonish the rest.**
>
> —*Mark Twain*
> *1835 – 1910*
> *Author and humorist*

Write down three of your "I believe" statements:

1　　I believe:

_____

_____

_____

2　　I believe:

_____

_____

_____

3　　I believe:

_____

_____

_____

> **"**Religion is for people who don't want to go to hell. Spirituality is for people who have already been through it.**"**
>
> —*Sister Joan Chittister*
> *Author and lecturer*

Will speaks:

"Find something in life larger than yourself in which to believe".

—*Will Keim*

Take an hour of power each day.

Every day, try to reserve thirty minutes for exercise followed by thirty minutes for prayer, reflection, meditation, or contemplation. This hour a day will:

- **Reenergize you.**
- **Recreate you.**
- **Revitalize you.**

You say, "I don't have an hour each day."
We say, "Then stress out."

> **The best thing about the future is that it comes one day at a time.**
>
> *—Abraham Lincoln*
> *1809 – 1865*
> *U.S. president*

Myth: "I don't have time. Other people have more time than I do."

Fact: Everybody gets twenty-four hours, seven days a week. Everybody.

What do you do with your 24 hours?

Okay, let's keep this real. You say you don't have time to take an hour out for exercise and contemplation? Take our "Keep it Real Challenge." Using the chart below, keep track of one day in your life and see where your time goes. Be honest. Be real.

Morning

5 – 6: _____

6 – 7: _____

7 – 8: _____

8 – 9: _____

9 – 10: _____

10 – 11: _____

11 – 12: _____

Noon

12 – 1: _____

1 – 2: _____

2 – 3: _____

3 – 4: _____

4 – 5: _____

5 – 6: _____

6 – 7: _____

7 – 8: _____

8 – 9: _____

9 – 10: _____

10 – 11: _____

11 – 12: _____

Midnight

12 – 1: _____

1 – 2: _____

2 – 3: _____

3 – 4: _____

4 – 5: _____

**Step 1 to good time management
is knowing how you spend your time.**

Sum it up.

Review your "Keep it Real" chart and total the number of hours you
spend on each activity:

Class: _____

Lab: _____

Study: _____

Eating: _____

Athletics: _____

Meetings: _____

Meditation: _____

Prayer: _____

Sleep: _____

Work: _____

Goofin' around: _____

Other:

_____: _____

_____: _____

TOTAL: _____

(Must equal 24 hours!)

Make some changes.

Just because you've always done it one way, does not mean you
can't change. Step out of old habits. Step out of the shadow of your
parents, big sister or brother, past achievements, and even defeats and
self doubts. Step into the light that is your life. Your moment. Your
collegiate experience.

Now is a great opportunity to identify and develop greater meaning
and purpose in your life.

List some changes that you'd like to consider:

_____

_____

_____

_____

_____

_____

_____

> **"Nothing endures
> but change."**
>
> —*Heraclitus*
> *540 – 480 BC*
> *Greek philosopher*

Character Lesson 7

Freedom

> 66 I quit drinking because I didn't want to be 'that guy.' That guy who was a jerk. That guy who woke up each morning thinking, 'Whom do I have to apologize to today?' That guy nice women avoided. 99
>
> —*Senior*
> *University of North Dakota*

Be free from dependence

Will stood in front of 2,000 students at Oregon State University to conduct a memorial service for a young fraternity man who died after falling, drunk, and hitting his head on a boat at Lake Shasta, California. His fraternity brothers tried to save him, but by the time they found him on the bottom of the lake, he was gone.

This event and others like it have prompted Will to speak out strongly to students: "I ask you to be free from dependence on alcohol and other drugs. I affirm your right not to drink, but I ask that, if you do drink, please be responsible and safe. When you are not, then people like me—ministers, priests, rabbis, imams—stand in sadness. No parent should outlive their child. No friend should be haunted with such a memory. Please, be free from dependence. Practice low- or no-risk drinking. Your life and the lives of your precious, wonderful friends depend on it."

Freedom
Spirit
Health
Character
Peacemaking
Service
Scholarship

> **Curtis speaks:**
> "I was a mime on cruise ships for several years. The entertainers did only three shows a week, so we had plenty of free time. I knew some people whose weekly bar bill on board ranged from $300 to $500 a week. *A week!* During that time, I met my wife, a singer and dancer for the cruise line. I am very glad that we were sober enough to recognize our love for each other."
> **Don't miss out on the good times.**
>
> —*Curtis Zimmerman*

Finding freedom

Many nations struggle with freedom from tyranny, despots, autocratic rulers, or brutal repression. For some, freedom of speech, assembly, religion, and even the choice of your own occupation or spouse are dream-like fantasies. Freedom draws a significant percentage of the world's immigrants to the shores of North America.

In North America freedom is a basic right. Why then do so many of our own citizens choose to live their lives in dependency on alcohol and other drugs? They surrender their freedom and give up control of their lives to something outside of themselves. Do you come from a home where alcohol or other drug abuse has damaged relationships, caused misery or even death? Many of us have.

Who are you fooling?

Abraham Lincoln was wrong when he said, "You can't fool all the people all the time." Sure you can. But the one person you cannot fool is yourself. Please do not feel that we are judging you. That is not our intent. Do feel invited to take an honest look at what you put into your body—particularly in terms of alcohol and other drugs.

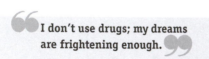

I don't use drugs; my dreams are frightening enough.

—*M.C. Escher*
1898 – 1972
Artist, famous for his "self-referential" art

Personal honesty

In his book *Sick and Tired of Being Sick and Tired*, author Philip L. Hansen writes, "It seems in this country whenever someone mentions alcohol, people either get mad or thirsty."

Do you get mad or thirsty? Some of you can drink socially and some of you can't. We are not advocating Prohibition II. We are asking for personal honesty, and we are offering a Personal Drinking Inventory that will guide you as you make alcohol-related choices in college.

Personal Drinking Inventory

How many drinks do you have per week?

- ☐ **0 drinks per week**
- ☐ **1–5 drinks per week**
- ☐ **6–10 drinks per week**
- ☐ **11–15 drinks per week**
- ☐ **16+ drinks per week**

Why include a Personal Drinking Inventory in a character lesson on freedom? Because by "freedom" we mean:

Freedom from dependence on alcohol and other drugs.
Freedom from addictions to nicotine and gambling.

So take a look at your PDI above.

Studies have shown an amazing relationship between drinks per week and grade point average: the higher the PDI drinks per week, the lower the grade point average. Higher PDIs are also related to missed classes and dropout rates.

You may say "I can handle it." All that should tell you is that you have built up a high tolerance—which isn't necessarily all that good either.

If you are drunk every weekend, you have a problem with alcohol.

The Good Book says that money is not the root of all evil. Rather, the love of money is the root of evil. Likewise, alcohol is not the cause of most student problems. *The abuse of alcohol* is the problem.

> **An American monkey after getting drunk on brandy would never touch it again, and thus is much wiser than most men.**
>
> —*Charles Darwin*
> *1809 – 1882*
> *Father of evolutionary biology*

Will speaks:

"I can't think of a single big mistake I made in college that wasn't alcohol related. I never missed a class in college because I was too sober. I never yelled an obscenity at the fraternity next door because I was too sober. I never cheated on my girlfriend because I was too sober. Every once in a while I think about all the time, and perhaps friends, I lost because of alcohol."

If you have problems when you drink, you are a problem drinker.

—*Will Keim*

The SAD Facts
(The Sex, Alcohol and Drug Connection)

The following numbers represent the percentage of these crimes or tragedies that are caused by alcohol and/or other drugs.

- ☐ 66% of all date/acquaintance rapes
- ☐ 41% of assaults
- ☐ 64% of homicides
- ☐ 60% of mental cruelty divorce cases
- ☐ 60% of suicide attempts
- ☐ 80% of dropouts

In addition:

- ☐ Alcohol-related car crashes kill 22,000 per year
- ☐ Alcohol is the #1 killer of men and women 18–24

Myth: Everyone drinks all the time.

Fact: 55% of students either don't drink or drink only 1–5 drinks per week.

Social Norming Theory makes the strong case that if students think "Everyone drinks. Everyone is having sex," the students will more likely behave in this perceived "norm." But the reality is most students drink responsibly or not at all; and a significant percentage of students abstain from sex for religious, health, and personal safety and self-esteem issues.

Question:

Do you know which of your friends drink too much?

Bigger Question:

How many of you know someone who has been killed in an alcohol- or drug-related accident?

Answer:

Too many of you.

Know the law.
Know your limit.
Know yourself.

> " [Social Norming Theory] holds that if students perceive something to be the norm, they tend to alter their behavior to fit that norm, even if it isn't reality. If, however, they are presented with the actual norm, they will conform to it. So, if students think heavy drinking is normal, they'll drink more. If they think responsible drinking is normal, they'll drink more responsibly. "
>
> *—Michael Haines*
> *Northern Illinois University*

Designer or club drugs

Methylenedioxymethamphetamin (MDMA or Ecstasy), Gamma-hydroxybutyric acid (GHB), Rohypnol, ketamine, methamphetamine. Big names for some serious drugs. They are just a few of the designer or club drugs showing up on campus, at "raves," dance clubs, and bars. These drugs can cause serious health problems and, in some cases, death. Used in combination with alcohol, they can be even more dangerous.

Date rape

You need to be aware of the horrific use of these drugs on campus. GHB and Rohypnol, for example, have been used in cases of date rape. Because you can't taste or smell GHB, it can be slipped into your drink or even put on your food without detection. Rohypnol, when mixed with alcohol, can incapacitate and prevent you from resisting sexual assault. Take care of yourself and your friends.

> " If we burn ourselves out with drugs or alcohol, we won't have long to go in this business. "
>
> —*John Belushi*
> *1949 – 1982*
> *Entertainer who died*
> *of a drug overdose*

Important:
Do not leave food or a beverage of any kind unattended at a party. If you feel light-headed, warm, or nauseous, find a same-sex friend to take you home.

Designer or club drugs adversely affect memory. If you can't remember the party, your date, what happened, or where your keys are, seek professional help.

Marijuana

The rules all changed in 1990 when Congress passed a law called the 1990 Drug Free Campus and Community Act, which says any drugs used within a mile of any school doubles the penalty upon conviction. What was a misdemeanor for our generation is a felony for your generation. That means on all your future job applications you will have to check the "YES" box when asked:

Have you been convicted of a drug-related offense or a felony?

Drugs? Think of them as an unemployment facilitator.
You're smarter than that.

Up in smoke

While we're talking about drugs, we can't forget nicotine. College
students are the leading users of tobacco products today, with the
number of smokers continuing to increase. According to a survey
from the Core Institute, 35.5 percent of college students in the
United States reported using tobacco within a one-month period.
Many students identify themselves as "social smokers." Social
smokers? Give us a break. Cigarettes contain nicotine, a drug that
is as addictive as heroin or cocaine, according to the Royal College
of Physicians. Just ask someone who has ever tried to quit. We have
sympathy for people who got hooked fifty years ago — before the
long-term health consequences of tobacco were known. But today,
you have no excuse. If you choose to smoke or chew tobacco, you are
putting a cancer-causing substance in your body. Pure and simple.
And besides, tobacco makes you smell bad. Who wants to kiss
an ash tray?

Hold 'em or fold 'em?

We came across the following statement from a college freshman at
Syracuse University: "Each month, my parents give me $300, and
right afterwards you can find me online gambling or at a casino.
All in all, I would say **I've lost at least $2,500, which more than
emptied my graduation savings account**."

Losing your graduation savings account to gambling is a sure-fire sign
that you have a gambling problem. Rick Barnes, an expert in college
student affairs and a well-known speaker, offers this insight:

"For most, gambling can be fun and entertaining. For some, it can
be a devastating illness that negatively affects every aspect of their
lives. Referred to as 'the hidden addiction,' compulsive gambling is
a challenge for some gamblers, carrying the same kinds of negative
consequences as drug or alcohol addiction. Compulsive gamblers
come from all walks of life. One cannot be too smart, too old, too
young, too successful, too religious, or too good of a student to
develop a gambling problem."

Barnes (barnes@campuspeak.com, 817-788-5019) has these suggestions if you choose to gamble:

- **Pre-determine the amount of money you plan to gamble prior to the outing.**
- **Take breaks at least every thirty minutes during a gambling outing.**
- **Avoid taking ATM or credit cards into the casino.**
- **Remain focused on why you are in college in the first place — make grades, pass classes and graduate.**

Problem Gambling Quiz

If you are concerned about your gambling, take this short quiz:

YES NO

☐ ☐ **Do you have an inability to stop gambling once you start?**

☐ ☐ **Do you set "loss limits" for the day and then routinely exceed them?**

☐ ☐ **Do you borrow money to pay gambling debts?**

☐ ☐ **Do you lie to friends or family about your gambling frequency or the extent of your losses?**

☐ ☐ **Do you neglect other responsibilities, such as school, because of a preoccupation with gambling?**

☐ ☐ **Do you constantly worry about your gambling?**

If you answered "YES" to any of these questions, it's time to get some help.

If you or someone you know needs help, contact the National Helpline for the National Council on Problem Gambling, (800) 522-4700 or *www.ncpgambling.org*.

> **[Problem gambling is a] progressive addiction characterized by an increasing preoccupation with gambling, a need to bet more money more frequently, restlessness or irritability when attempting to stop, "chasing" losses, and loss of control manifested by continuation of the gambling behavior in spite of mounting, serious, negative consequences.**
>
> —*National Council on Problem Gambling*

Character Lesson 8

Letting Go

> **When I was 14 I thought my father was ignorant. By the time I was 21 I was amazed how much he had learned in seven years.**
>
> —*Mark Twain*
> *1835 – 1910*
> *Author and humorist*

Living your own life

"I hate chemistry," the student said to her counselor. "I hate it, and I have failed it three times. But I have to take it to be a dietician." Her counselor looked puzzled. "Is that what you want to be?" he asked. "No. But my mom was a dietician, and I don't want to disappoint her."

"Does she want you to be one?" he asked. The student's face crinkled up as she pondered the question. "I think so."

"Why don't you call her? Now." He handed his phone to the student who punched in her mom's number. The tears started to fall. She told her mom thanks and hung up. The student turned to her counselor. "My mom said she just wants me to be happy. Whatever major makes me happy is fine with her."

Are you majoring in something because of your parents, because of a trend, or because you love it? Do the right thing for the right reason. Both students and parents have to let go at some point and allow each other to live their lives.

Letting Go
Freedom
Spirit
Health
Character
Peacemaking
Service
Scholarship

> **Will speaks:**
> "I know a soccer player from the University of New Hampshire whose father went to all her games. Watching their exchange of love and respect after a game was great. She is blessed. So here it is: Your parents did the best they could. Most of them parented you the way they were parented by their folks. Perhaps that New Hampshire dad had a father who went to all of his games. "
> **What kind of parents do you have?**
>
> —*Will Keim*

Walls

The Great Wall of China was built to keep marauding armies and unwanted cultures out. The Berlin Wall was built to separate East Germany and West Germany; it also separated brothers and sisters, parents and children. The goodness or badness of a wall largely rests in the eye of the beholder.

Here is some information that generally gets left out of the collegiate educational experience:

- **Some of you were blessed with great parents.**
- **Some of you were not.**

It is time to make a "Big Choice" regarding your parents. You have two choices:

Choice 1

If you are angry at your parents, begin the healing and forgiving process by letting go of your anger. If you let it eat you up, then the anger wins. Their problem becomes your problem.

Choice 2

If you have a good relationship, thank your parents for doing a great job—especially if you have a single parent who did a great job. Those parents are saints. For single parents or guardians, this is the picture: WORK • WORK • CARE GIVE • PARENT • WORK • COOK • SLEEP • WORK SOME MORE • PARENT • SLEEP

> "There are two lasting bequests we can give our children. One is roots. The other is wings. "
>
> —*Hodding Carter, Jr.*
> *1907 – 1972*
> *Journalist*

Assignment:

Write a letter to your parents. Share the most important lesson they have taught you. Pretend that after this letter, for whatever reason, you will not be able to speak directly with them again. Please hand-write the letter after five minutes of quiet reflection.

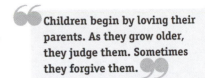

Children begin by loving their parents. As they grow older, they judge them. Sometimes they forgive them.

—*Author unknown*

Dear _____

Sincerely,

_____

The wise path

Your parents will, in the best-case scenario, become your friends and trusted mentors or advisors. As you have your own family, your parents will become grandparents and valuable assistants in the raising of your own children.

Then one day it will dawn on you that you are taking care of your parents, or not. The quality of their health care and later years will largely be determined by their relationship to you. It makes good sense to make peace with them now. Thank them if you can. Forgive them if you can't. Let go of the past, and get on with the present. This is the wise path to take with your parents.

Remember: Going to college is not just a big step for you, but also for your parents.

Curtis speaks:

"In order to make room for new things in your life, you must first let go of some old, limiting beliefs about yourself. I used to see myself as a kid on welfare who would always be sick, in the hospital, with little to contribute. Now I see myself as a healthy husband, father, and teacher sharing life-changing messages. My new beliefs and actions are much more productive and empowering."
How do you see yourself?

—*Curtis Zimmerman*

List a few things that you'd like to let go:

_____

_____

_____

_____

_____

_____

_____

_____

_____

Will speaks:

"There is both conceptual and experiential knowledge in life. I can tell you not to go over Niagara Falls in a barrel, not because I have done it but because I have stood at the top of the Falls and can conceptualize the damage or death the fall might incur. With parenting it is different. You have to experience it to understand it. As a student you either have to thank you parents for a job well done or begin the healing process by letting-go of the anger for a job not so well done by them. There is no other way. Don't let your parent's problems and shortcomings become your problems and your issues. Get help if you need it because this is your life to live."

—Will Keim, Son & Parent

> I talk and talk and talk, and I haven't taught people in 50 years what my father taught by example in one week.
>
> *—Mario Cuomo*
> *1932 –*
> *Former governor of New York*

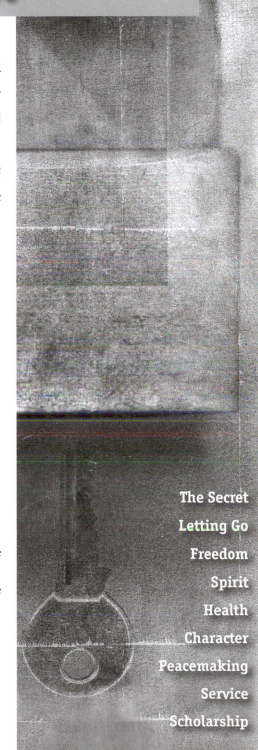

Character Lesson 9

The Secret

> ❝To love what you do and feel that it matters— how could anything be more fun?❞

—Katherine Graham
1917 – 2001
Publisher, The Washington Post

Saving a life

When Curtis was twelve years old he used to walk to a nearby shopping mall in Torrance, California, to play video games. For Curtis, the mall was a respite from the chaos of his home life. One Saturday afternoon he saw a mime, called Tommy, in the mall performing a mechanical robot routine. Curtis stared—fascinated. That night all he did was practice the mechanical robot. For five weeks, Curtis followed Tommy. Everywhere he went in the mall, Curtis followed and watched. (They call this stalking, now.) Every night Curtis practiced the routine. Finally, he gathered his courage to speak to Tommy. "I can do what you do!" he said. "Well, little man, let's see," Tommy replied. Curtis did his robot routine. When he was finished, Tommy said, "Come back tomorrow."

The next day, Tommy had gathered some of the mall executives. "Show them," he said to Curtis, so Curtis did his routine. When he finished, Tommy said to the executives, "I want you to hire him this summer. I will teach him." With a laugh they replied, "Tommy, you're one of the best mimes in all of Los Angeles. Why would we hire some kid off the street?" Tommy replied, "Because if you don't, I quit." "We have no budget," they said. Tommy leaned over and whispered, "Pay him $5 an hour and take it out of my pay." "Fine," they said as they walked away.

"Tommy saved my life that day," Curtis says today. "Tommy helped me discover myself and what I wanted to do with my life."

The Secret

Letting Go

Freedom

Spirit

Health

Character

Peacemaking

Service

Scholarship

Is there a better way?

Many people believe that the secret to life is money, riches, and wealth. Honestly, if we had to choose between poor and happy or rich and happy, we would choose the latter. But be clear: Money does not make people happy. If it did, then the United States would be the happiest place on earth. Yet we spend more than $150 billion a year on alcohol and import 150 metric tons of cocaine. If life is so good here, why do so many people live it sedated? Is there a better way? We have learned the secret of life, and we believe it can lead you to happiness and satisfaction with your college experience and beyond.

The Secret:

Find something you love to do and learn to do it well enough that people will pay you to do it.

Know what you love.
Do what you love.
The Secret to Life.

Meagan Denney speaks:

"I said earlier in the book that I found softball and it helped me develop confidence on the field and off. What is your softball? That is, what class, activity, or passion will you find that helps you find your self esteem and your way in college? Be creative. There is something for everyone on campus."

Seek, and you will find your softball.

—*Meagan Denney*

> **If one advances confidently in the direction of his dreams, and endeavors to live the life which he has imagined, he will meet with a success unexpected in common hours.**
>
> —*Henry David Thoreau*
> *1817 – 1862*
> *Author, poet, philosopher*

Choose a major

To choose an appropriate major, complete the following chart. The
first example is how Nora might have filled it out.

What I love	Relevant Major(s)	Potential Job(s)
Example: *Writing* *Photography* *Design*	*Communications* *Journalism*	*Newspaper reporter* *Graphic artist* *Magazine editor*

Go through the course catalog with a yellow marker. Highlight all the
classes that interest you. See what major they add up to.

Will speaks:

"In college I was ridiculed by two classmates for being a speech major. They were business majors. 'Business—that's where the bucks are,' one told me. 'What are you going to do with a speech major—travel around the county giving speeches?' he added with a laugh. Those guys went to work for Enron. And I, indeed, ended up traveling around the country giving speeches. While I was hanging out with college students, they were hanging out with greedy, future felons. While I was visiting university campuses, they were visiting courtrooms. While I still love what I do, they are both unemployed (and one is in jail)."

Do what you love.

—*Will Keim*

> **Success is the peace of mind that comes from knowing you did the best you were capable of doing, and you are the only one who will ever know that.**
>
> —*John Wooden*
> *1910 –*
> *Retired UCLA basketball coach who won 10 NCAA championships*

Take your own path

Will's story is not meant to belittle business majors. By all means, major in business if you want. But do it because you love it—not because "that's where the bucks are," or because your father wants you to, or because someone else tells you it's hot.

What is the path you are on?

_____

_____

_____

_____

_____

_____

_____

_____

Where would you like to go?

_____

_____

_____

_____

_____

_____

_____

_____

_____

_____

> **The future is not a result of choices among alternative paths offered by the present, but a place that is created—created first in the mind and will, created next in activity. The future is not some place we are going to, but one we are creating. The paths are not to be found, but made, and the activity of making them changes both the maker and the destination.**
>
> —*John Schaar*
> *Futurist and Professor Emeritus*
> *University of California Santa Cruz*

'Sometimes they are wrong'

Despite the objections of many, the actor and director Kevin Costner insisted that the Native Americans speak their own language in his 1990 film "Dances with Wolves."

"People will always tell you what to do with your life. That's called conventional wisdom," Costner said when questioned about his decision. "Sometimes they are wrong. Follow your heart."

The movie won seven Academy Awards including Best Picture.

Character Lesson 10

25,000 Days

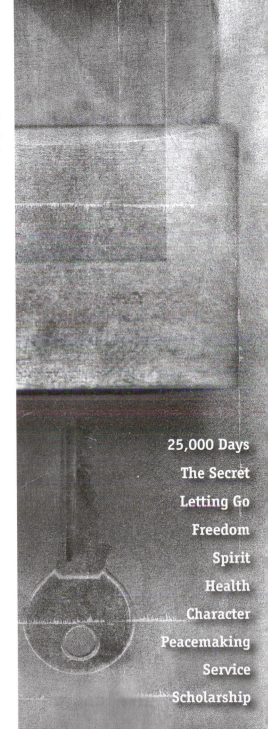

> The quality of a person's life is in direct proportion to their commitment to excellence, regardless of their chosen field of endeavor.
>
> —*Vince Lombardi*
> *1913 – 1970*
> *Coach, Green Bay Packers*

Making every day count

Most of us will get about 70 years of life. At least that's what the National Center for Health Statistics says. Some of us will live longer; some will live less. It all depends on your gender, genes, geography, and other factors. Of course, we all think that we'll be the ones to get a few more years. But think about it: Chances are you know someone your own age who has already died. Ryan White, who was born a hemophiliac, contracted AIDS from a blood transfusion at age 13. He was given six months to live. At the time, the American public understood little about AIDS, and, in the absence of knowledge, fear of the disease prevailed. Ryan was persecuted—school officials tried to bar him from attending, restaurants denied him access, vandals painted "FAG" on his school locker. Ryan defied the odds and lived five years after contracting AIDS. He spent those years working to reduce prejudice against people living with AIDS. He was tireless in his efforts to educate the general public. He became famous. Hollywood made a movie of his life. A recent Google search for "Ryan White" yielded 7.8 million hits, ranging from a national youth conference to a journalism award named in his honor. Ryan died at age 18—52 years short of what he might have expected.

25,000 Days

The Secret

Letting Go

Freedom

Spirit

Health

Character

Peacemaking

Service

Scholarship

Death denying

Scholars Elizabeth Kübler Ross and Dr. Marcus Borg describe our culture as "death denying." What do they mean? We routinely depict death in movies and television shows, but most of the time death is depicted as a horrific event. In reality, most people die quietly at home. We do not want to think about that, so we throw in a chain saw, ghouls, bats, bees, huge spiders, aliens, and a host of other horrible things that we will most likely never see. The point is this: When we see a huge spider grab a guy we think, "Wow, that'll never happen to me." If we present death as it really is, we would be moved to say, "That is exactly what's going to happen to me."

"Death is the ultimate teacher," said the philosopher Søren Kierkegaard. It should be, and it should keep us busy and moving.

When we avoid death by sending all our old people away to live separately from us or deny it with endless plastic surgeries, we are wearing blinders. When breast, lip and nose jobs become routine, when we label everything "NEW" as if that makes it better, then we are clearly living in a death-denying, youth-focused, elder-phobic society.

So what?

You might be inclined to say, "So what? I'm young. What does this have to do with me? I'm just getting ready to start my life."

You may not be as young as you think. Just as "I'll do it later" usually translates to "It won't get done," "I've got all the time in the world" really indicates a lack of understanding the most important point of this lesson:

The day you were born, you had 25,000 days left.

Did you know that 25,000 grains of sand will fit into your two hands? That's not a lot. 25,000 days—that's if you live a *full* life. If you have prostate cancer, heart disease, or breast cancer in your family, you may get less than 25,000. Singer Selena got 8,744 days. Distance runner Steve Prefontaine got 8,885 days. Ryan White got 6,693 days.

So, here's the wake-up call:
An 18-year-old has already used up
about 6,500 days—that leaves 18,500 days.

> " I look to the future because that's where I'm going to spend the rest of my life. "
>
> —*George Burns*
> *1896 – 1996*
> *Entertainer*

How are you going to spend them? If you like the way your life is going, keep on doin' what you're doin'! But if you don't, now would be a great time to make some changes. Why wait? Need help? You've got a whole college or university standing by, including:

> Academic services
> Counseling services
> Tutors
> Health services
> Recreation
> Intramurals
> Food services
> Student activities
> Student involvement centers
> Campus ministries
> Intercollegiate athletics
> Club sports

> **And in the end, it's not the years in your life that count. It's the life in your years.**
>
> —*Abraham Lincoln*
> *1809 – 1865*
> *U.S. president*

It's all here. The only thing missing is you.

Your Task:

List your thoughts to the following two questions:

1 What are my three greatest accomplishments so far?

1. _____
2. _____
3. _____

2 What are ten things I want to do before I die?

1. _____
2. _____
3. _____
4. _____
5. _____
6. _____
7. _____
8. _____
9. _____
10. _____

Did you know? Head football coaches Lou Holtz and John L. Smith have a list of 100 things they want to do before they die.

> **Will speaks:**
>
> "His name was Roosevelt Andre Credit and he sang like an angel. I heard him singing in a Residence Hall Lounge to himself and invited him to come and sing at my Church. He sang 'Amazing Grace' with so much passion that people yelled 'Amen!'. This doesn't happen at our rather staid congregation. I asked him what his major was and he said, "Music education, sir." I said, "You should major in vocal performance. You have a gift." We discussed it for six months and finally he decided to give it a shot. "What are the chances of me earning my living singing?" "Slim and none." I said. "But I don't want you to have any regrets. Go for it."
>
> He has sung on Broadway in New York for ten years, traveled to Japan with the New York Ragtime Orchestra, and participated in the Duke Ellington Tribute at the Kennedy Center. He has private students and is the guest vocalist at major Church and philanthropic events in the City. He just needed a little nudge. A vote of confidence. He had all the skills but lacked the belief in self that is so essential to accomplish great things in life.
>
> What great things will you do if you find your passion and listen to the voice within you that says to you, "You can do it!" Stop listening to the voices of others that set limits for you that are below your capabilities. Form a plan, work the plan, and find something you love to do and learn to do it well enough that someone will pay you to do it. You will be happy and doing what you were put here to do!"
>
> —*Will Keim*

> 66 **Avoiding danger is no safer in the long run than outright exposure. The fearful are caught as often as the bold.** 99
>
> *—Helen Keller*
> *1880 – 1968*
> *Blind and deaf social activist*

Make a plan

Now it's time to plan. First, you need to learn the language you will use in your plan.

> **Dreams:** That's the big picture. Think big.
> **Goals:** These are the guidelines to help you actualize your dreams.
> **Objectives:** Specific ways to reach those goals and dreams.
> **Action Plan:** Nuts and bolts. The "How ya gonna do it."
> **Due Date:** Holds you accountable and lets you check your progress.

As you complete the plan on the next page, don't hold back. Be bold. Take a moment to reflect before you begin to write.

What is it you'd *really* like to do?
How can you make it happen?
What do you need to do to make that dream a reality?

Okay, get to it!

Your Task:

Make a plan to achieve your dream.

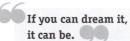

**If you can dream it,
it can be.**

—Walt Disney
1901 – 1966
Creator of the Disney empire

One dream:

1 _____

_____

_____

Two goals:

2 _____

_____

_____

_____

Three objectives:

3 _____

_____

_____

_____

_____

_____

Your plan:

_____

_____

_____

_____

_____

_____

By when:

_____

_____

_____

The remainder of your 25,000 days

Your final task for Lesson 10 is to write a Personal Mission Statement on how you envision the remainder of your 25,000 days. We know your mission statement will change over time. So why write one? For the same reason you wash your hands—even knowing they will get dirty again. It's the right thing to do.

Your statement can include, but is not limited to:

- **Your philosophy of life**
- **Intentions**
- **Dreams**
- **Goals**
- **Objectives**
- **Action plans**
- **Timelines**
- **Beliefs**
- **Attitudes**
- **Values**
- **Commitments**

Try starting your Personal Mission Statement with
"I see myself ..."
"I will ..."
"I believe ..."
"I promise to ..."

> **The tragedy of life is not that it ends so soon, but that we wait so long to begin it.**
>
> —*Author unknown*

Personal Mission Statement

Date: _____

_____

_____

_____

_____

_____

_____

_____

_____

_____

_____

_____

_____

_____

_____

_____

_____

_____

_____

> **When you were born, you cried and the world rejoiced. Live your life so that when you die, the world cries and you rejoice.**
>
> —*Native American saying*

_____

_____

_____

_____

Signed:

_____

Character Lesson 11

Living Your Life at Performance Level

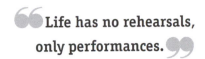

Life has no rehearsals, only performances.

—*Author unknown*

Attitude

Olympic gold medalist Carol Schaudt played only one season of basketball at a community college before she came to Oregon State University. "I was totally ignorant of the game," she admits. "The only thing that even got me noticed was my 6'4" frame." Given her lack of knowledge of the sport, she put her faith in her new OSU coach, Aki Hill. Carol remembers thinking: *If I just do what I am told by my coach, I will become successful.* One of the first things Coach Hill told Carol was that missing a shot was unacceptable. *Make 100 percent of my shots?* Carol thought. That seemed extreme to her, but if the coach expected it, then it must be possible.

Carol worked hard at her shooting, doing everything Coach Hill told her to do. By her senior year, she led the nation in both points per game (averaging almost 29), and field-goal percentage (exactly 75 percent). "It was not just about technique; it was mostly about attitude," she says now. "Reflecting back, I realize that I never shot a shot that I didn't think I was going to make. It's true that I fell short of my goal of shooting 100 percent, but do you think I would have averaged 75 percent if my goal had been to shoot 50 percent?"

Living Your Life at Performance Level

25,000 Days

The Secret

Letting Go

Freedom

Spirit

Health

Character

Peacemaking

Service

Scholarship

Bit part or star?

Unaware as most folks are that they have just some portion of 25,000 days to live, they seek bit parts in other people's shows (lives) and settle for a role out of the light, where they can blend in and not take responsibility for the play (their life). We'd like you to consider living your life at performance level. It means you will:

- Be the director of your own life.
- Define your own character.
- Write your own script.
- Select your own supporting cast.
- Practice.
- Be the star in your life.

You have two choices:

1 You can choose to be the "Director of Your Life" and the "Star of Your Show"; or

2 You can choose to play the "Victim of Your Life" and never have a starring role.

> In high school, I was the class comedian as opposed to the class clown. The difference is, the class clown is the guy who drops his pants at the football game, the class comedian is the guy who talked him into it.
>
> —Billy Crystal
> 1947 –
> Entertainer

Curtis speaks:

"For twenty-five years I earned my living as a mime, fire eater, unicyclist, juggler, and magician. I wrote my scripts, cast my show wisely, and rehearsed—all to prepare for opening day. One day I realized everything I had to do to mount a show for Universal Studios was exactly what I had to do to live my Real Life at performance level. I had to write my own life script, select the people I wanted in my life (my supporting cast), and practice life skills. I also realized that every day that I open my eyes is opening day."

Be the director of your own life.

—*Curtis Zimmerman*

Write *out* some characters

When we suggest that you "select supporting cast members for your life's play," we also mean you should write *out* some existing "characters" in your life. Are there people in your life who only make life more difficult for you? Write them *out* of your life—or at least minimize the number of lines you give them. Some people in your life have way too many lines.

Will speaks:

"A very wise hockey coach told me there are three types of people: *Prolongers*: They just keep doing things the same old way even if it isn't working. *Protesters*: They rebel against any new idea because they fear change. *Proactives*: They take what works from the past, what makes sense from the new, and boldly step forward.

"I told him I thought he was right on target. I shared with him my theory that you can motivate people with a carrot, a hug, or a kick in the pants. The key to successful motivation is knowing which tool to use."

Be proactive in your life. Know what motivates you.

—*Will Keim*

Motivation

Everybody is different when it comes to motivation. Understanding what motivates you will help you live life at performance level. For example, an entertainer may thrive on recognition; the possibility of a standing ovation motivates him to rework his comedy sketch until it's just perfect. A scientist may be driven by the idea of discovering something that no one has ever thought of; she works in the laboratory for years motivated by that goal.

> **Ability is what you're capable of doing. Motivation determines what you do. Attitude determines how well you do it.**
>
> —*Lou Holtz*
> *1937 –*
> *Football coach*

What will motivate you to live life at performance level?

Check all that apply:
- ☐ **Feeling like I've made a difference.**
- ☐ **Being appreciated.**
- ☐ **A paycheck.**
- ☐ **Having room to be creative.**
- ☐ **Good grades.**
- ☐ **Power. Being in charge.**
- ☐ **Recognition.**
- ☐ **Being the best.**
- ☐ **Other:**

_____

_____

Three Basic Assumptions About Life
.1 Life is not a dress rehearsal.
.2 You have a finite number of days to live and an infinite number of experiences.
.3 It is time for you to be the star of the show entitled "Your Life."

> We all use our imagination every day. However, most of us are unaware that what we envision affects every cell of our bodies and every aspect of our performance.
>
> —*Marilyn King*
> *Two-time Olympian*
> *1972, 1976*

Why would you think that you could:

- Coast throughout the semester, yet expect to get "A's"?
- Treat people poorly, and then one day treat your spouse with dignity and respect?
- Not get involved on campus, yet expect a great job or winning resume to magically appear?

Write your script:

- Adventure? Comedy? Tragedy? Love story? Drama?

Select your supporting cast:

- Do the people around you help you stand in the spotlight or drag you backstage into the dark?

Prepare for opening day:

- Practice, and don't be afraid to be the star of your show.

Let's recap:

Using the chart on the next page, write down a few potential scripts for your life. Include your cast and the outcomes.

Potential Scripts	Supporting Cast	Outcomes
EXAMPLE: *Adventure! Keep taking photography classes. Intern this summer at The Nature Conservancy magazine. Practice my Spanish. Take pictures daily.*	*Mom, Dad, Riley, Ben, Bruce, Professor Little, Mr. D'Ambroso, Uncle Bob, Dr. Main, Kathie, Frank. Fewer lines to: Sam, Andrea. Write out completely: Kurt.*	*Staff photographer for a wildlife magazine. Eventually become a freelance photographer with emphasis on endangered species in South America.*

**Character
Lesson 12**

Learning to
Fail Successfully

> ❝ **I tried and failed.
> I tried again and didn't fail.** ❞
>
> —*Gail Borden, Jr.*
> *1801 – 1874*
> *Founder, Borden Dairy Products*

The process

Abraham Lincoln lost ten elections, but was elected to the one at
the right time that saved our country. Scott Joplin died without the
public's recognition of his genius, yet today his music is still played as
the finest of the Ragtime era. Sheryl Crow sang in virtual anonymity
for twenty years before critics came to believe in her as much as
she always had. Billy Mills grew up on a reservation and was called
horrible things when he went to the university, but he hung in there
and won a gold medal at the Tokyo Olympics. Jennifer Capriati
overcame a host of personal problems to become one of the world's
best tennis players.

Successful people have failed more than people who are considered
failures. Failing is not just part of the process. It *is* the process.

Learning to
Fail Successfully

Living Your Life at
Performance Level

25,000 Days

The Secret

Letting Go

Freedom

Spirit

Health

Character

Peacemaking

Service

Scholarship

Knocked down

Several years ago an Australian rock group offered this anthem for learning to fail successfully:

**"I get knocked down, but I get up again,
nobody gonna keep me down."**

Did you ever feel like you were:
- Knocked down?
- Used?
- Lied to?
- Bullied?
- Made fun of?

If you've been knocked down, get up, and learn to fail successfully. Until you understand this one, simple teaching, you are doomed to underachieve your potential:

The key to success is failure.

> **Good people are good because they've come to wisdom through failure.**
>
> —*William Saroyan*
> *1908 – 1981*
> *Novelist*

Curtis speaks:

"I was hospitalized thirty-seven times by my ninth birthday. For unknown reasons, I was very anemic and had seizures much of my childhood. At age sixteen, I was terribly sick and hospitalized again. But this time I met a doctor determined to find out what caused my illness. For nearly three months I lay in the hospital while he ran test after test. On the plus side, I could eat whatever I wanted, and pancakes were my favorite. One morning, my doctor came into my room, grabbed my plate of pancakes and threw them on the floor. 'Curtis, you'll never eat pancakes again,' he said. 'We figured it out. You have a rare disease called Celiac, and the cure is easy. All you have to do is stop eating wheat, rye, oats and barley for the rest of your life, and you'll be great!'

"I gave up my pancakes (and bread and pasta and beer and ...), and in return, I received a happy and healthy life. Thank goodness that doctor did not give up on me."
Don't give up.

—*Curtis Zimmerman*

Perseverance

We received the following letter from a student who heard Will speak. Will's message about not giving up resonated with this young man. In fact, he had already learned the lesson himself. Read on:

> **Mistakes are the portals of discovery.**
>
> —James Joyce
> *1882 – 1941*
> *Writer*

"My freshman year of high school was the worst year of my life. Instead of doing homework, I was sneaking out to go drinking. By winter break I was taking drugs and drinking nightly. My grades fell to below a 'D' average.

"At the end of the year, most of my friends had been either expelled or sent to military schools. My parents moved me to a new high school where my mother worked so she could keep an eye on me. With the help of my parents and my football coaches, I was able to turn my life around. My grades rose to a 'C+' average, and my parents encouraged me to apply to colleges.

"My guidance counselor, however, told me that I didn't have what it took to succeed at college; she suggested I look into trade schools. I was determined to prove her wrong, and I applied to ten colleges. I was rejected by all ten. I was heart broken but refused to quit.

"My mom suggested I apply to the University of Redlands, but I was denied again. I appealed the decision. A few weeks later the admission host called and offered me an opportunity. 'Attend community college for 24 units,' he said, 'and if you can maintain a 3.00 GPA, we will admit you.' I took the challenge, succeeded, and was admitted to Redlands where I have done well. I plan to become a high school history teacher.

"I failed many times in my life, but it all made me a stronger person. It took me thirteen applications and a year in community college to be admitted into a four-year university, but with the support of my parents and my mentors, I have persevered.

"One of the greatest delights in my life is that I proved my guidance counselor wrong."

—*Steven Burke*

> **Will speaks:**
> "I applied for 23 jobs out of Graduate School and armed with a Master's Degree, I was rejected 23 times. 100% failure. The 24th school, Whittier College, hired me! It was at Whittier College that I met Donna Basham, my wife of 30 years and the Mother of our four children. Suddenly, everything made sense. Believe in yourself and never give up hope."
>
> —*Will Keim*

Give yourself

5,000 Tries

before you decide you can't do something (like juggle).

5,000 Tries

before you quit school.

5,000 Tries

before you accept defeat.

5,000 Tries

before you accept the life you are living (unless you already love it!)

> **Life's real failure is when you do not realize how close you were to success when you gave up.**
>
> —*Author unknown*

Wake-Up Exercise

List three things that you've given up on that you commit to try again:

1 _____

2 _____

3 _____

A final note

When we say "Don't give up," we need to add one qualifier: Each time you try again, try it a little differently. That's called learning. Curtis's doctor did not keep running the same test over and over; he tried one different test after another. Steven Burke, the student who wrote to us about getting into college, realized he could not just keep sending out college applications; he learned *why* colleges were rejecting him and changed. During Nora's attempts to get her book published, she researched publishers that would be most likely to accept a manuscript like hers; she rewrote her submission cover letter many times based on cover letters that had been successful.

Advertising guru Joseph Sugarman sums it up this way: "Not many people are willing to give failure a second opportunity. They fail once and it is all over. The bitter pill of failure is often more than most people can handle. If you are willing to accept failure and learn from it, if you are willing to consider failure as a blessing in disguise and bounce back, you will harness one of the most powerful success forces."

> **In order to succeed you must fail, so that you know what not to do the next time.**
>
> *—Anthony J. D'Angelo*
> *from* The College Blue Book

Put it all together

Review/Resources

> **Some men and women make the world better just by being the kind of people they are.**
>
> *—John W. Gardner*
> *1912 – 2002*
> *Leader, activist, reformer*

One more time...

Be scholars, servants, and peacemakers. Men and women of character, whose good health is mental, physical, and spiritual. Be free from dependence on alcohol, nicotine or other drugs, and gambling. Thank your parents or forgive them for not being perfect. Know that the secret of college life is to find something you love to do and learn to do it well enough that someone will pay you to do it. You have 18,500 days left to make your masterpiece by living life at performance level and learning to fail successfully.

Learning to
Fail Successfully

Living Your Life at
Performance Level

25,000 Days

The Secret

Letting Go

Freedom

Spirit

Health

Character

Peacemaking

Service

Scholarship

Build your own
'Plan for Success'

Below is a review of all twelve character lessons. In the chart on the next page, write a few words about how each lesson applies to you. Make notes of any actions you plan to take to put the lessons to work. Writing things down helps you remember them.

Character Lesson	Key Message
Learning to Fail Successfully	The key to success is failure. Don't give up.
Living Your Life at Performance Level	Write your own script for your life. Be the star. Who are your supporting characters?
25,000 Days	Make every day count. You only have 18,500 days left.
The Secret	Find something you love to do and learn to do it well enough that people will pay you to do it.
Letting Go	Some of you were blessed with great parents. Some were not. Either thank or forgive them.
Freedom	Be free from dependence on alcohol, nicotine, and other drugs.
Spirit	Reserve one hour per day for exercise and quiet contemplation.
Health	Practice safer sex or abstain. Saying "no" is often the most "Response-Able" thing to say.
Character	Say what you mean. Do what you say. If you don't, admit it. Make amends, and move on.
Peacemaking	Make peace with yourself. Resolve conflict with others.
Service	Great learning takes place in the act of giving assistance to others.
Scholarship	Being a good student is the basis on which success must be built.

Character Lesson	How I can apply this lesson to my life:
Learning to Fail Successfully	
Living Your Life at Performance Level	
25,000 Days	
The Secret	
Letting Go	
Freedom	
Spirit	
Health	
Character	
Peacemaking	
Service	
Scholarship	

Will and Curtis speak:

We are pleased to leave you with two additional resources:

- Ten Characteristics of Effective Leadership
- Fifty Stress Busters for Students

During your collegiate career, you will hear and learn much about leadership, and you will certainly encounter stress on your journey. We hope that these resources will get you started off on the right foot.

Blessings,
Will Keim, Curtis Zimmerman,

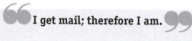

I get mail; therefore I am.

—*Scott Adams*
1957 –
"Dilbert" cartoonist

Want to keep in touch?

You can reach us through:

Will Keim Speaks!, Inc.
3850 NW Jackson
Corvallis, OR 97330
(800) 848-3897
www.willkeim.com

Zimmerman Productions
7577 Central Parke Blvd., Suite 217
Mason, OH 45040
(513) 229-3626
www.curtiszimmerman.com

E-mail IDs:
willkeim@att.net
curtis@curtiszimmerman.com

Ten Characteristics of Effective Leadership

Do you want to be a leader?
Do you want to make a difference?
Then here's how:

Learn to Listen ...
> To the voice within and the voices of others. Listen.

Empathy—develop it ...
> For the life history and needs of others. Feel.

Action ...
> Be the director, not the victim, of your life. Get busy.

Delegate ...
> Trust others to help you when you need assistance.
> Reach out.

Enthusiasm ...
> Get excited about yourself. Don't show up late for your life.

Reflection ...
> Think, meditate, prayer, ponder—pick one! Take time.

Stewardship ...
> Take care of yourself. Treat your life with the respect
> it deserves.

Humor ...
> Laugh at yourself and with others. Smile and enjoy.

Integrity ...
> Say what you mean, do what you say, and when you don't,
> admit it. Speak the truth.

Patience ...
> Give yourself and your friends a break. Let go of the past.
> Live now.

> **Leadership is the process of persuasion and example by which an individual or leadership team induces a group to take action that is in accord with the leader's purposes or the shared purposes of all.**
>
> *—John W. Gardner*
> *1912 – 2002*
> *Leader, activist, reformer*

Fifty Stress Busters for Students

1. **Be a scholar.** Read all your assignments.

2. **Go to class.** Life goes better if you show up.

3. **Re-copy your notes** every night in outline form to eliminate the unimportant stuff.

4. **Make a master syllabus.** Combine course syllabi into a megalist of all assignments.

5. **Maximize the missing minutes.** Study between classes during the day.

6. **See all your professors** at least once during office hours. Then, they can grade a person, not a number.

7. **See your advisor** at least once a term.

8. **Get involved.** Check out opportunities at the student center.

9. **Work out** in the campus rec center for thirty minutes every day.

10. **Play intramurals.** It's a great way to relax and meet people.

11. **Sleep 6-8 hours a night.** No one says you have to stay up all night.

12. **Eat breakfast every day.** Get it ... Break(the)fast.

13. **Get up 15 minutes** earlier each day. Avoid starting your day in a rush.

14. **Keep a to-do list** and daily planner. Structure gives freedom—really!

15. **Avoid procrastination.** Now!

16. **Think before you speak.** Be nice to your roommate.

17. **Don't sweat** the small stuff.

18. **Do good,** and be good to yourself and others.

19. **Listen more,** talk less.

20. **Set a realistic schedule** (daily/weekly/semester) and plan in rest breaks and time off.

21. **Focus on one thing** at a time. Do the least attractive stuff first.

22. **Volunteer some time** to charity or community service.

23. **Make friends** with a diverse group of people.

24. **Be kind** to unkind people; they need kindness the most.

25. **Cut people some slack.** Remember that everyone on campus is carrying some kind of heavy burden.

26. **When stressed, breathe** from your abdomen, not your chest. Deep and slow.

27. **Learn from the past;** live in the present; prepare for the future.

28. **Laugh** easily and often.

29. **Check your e-mail once** a day, not on the hour.

30. **Eat sensibly.** Only one third of your calories should come from fat.

31. **Say what you mean** and do what you say. When you don't, admit it.

32. **Make promises sparingly** and keep the ones you make.

33. **Be yourself.** Trends come and go.

34. **Delegate.** Let people help you and choose to help others.

35. **Eliminate or moderate** your intake of alcohol, caffeine, tobacco, and other drugs.

36. **Replace the word "problem"** with "opportunity."

37. **Do your best.** This will give you peace of mind.

38. **Practice humility** and random acts of kindness.

39. **See a counselor** if you need or want to see one.

40. **Forgive your parents** for not being perfect.

41. **Thank your parents** if they did a good job.

42. **Dream big dreams** about your success.

43. **Find something you love to do** and learn to do it well enough that you can get paid to do it .

44. **Go to the Career Planning** and Placement Services Center now! Avoid the rush.

45. **Keep a journal** with your victories and concerns.

46. **Keep a book by your bed** —one you read for pleasure before you go to sleep each night.

47. **Attend the spiritual service** of your choice or practice reflective quietude regularly.

48. **Be patient** with yourself and others.

49. **Be enthusiastic** and develop your sense of humor.

50. **Celebrate your attendance** at the university by smiling at people on campus.

Notes

Notes